Sheffield Tr

2023-2024.

A Traveller's Guide to the Steel City

Tarisha Sanchez

Sheffiel travel guide guide 2023-2024.

Map of Beighton

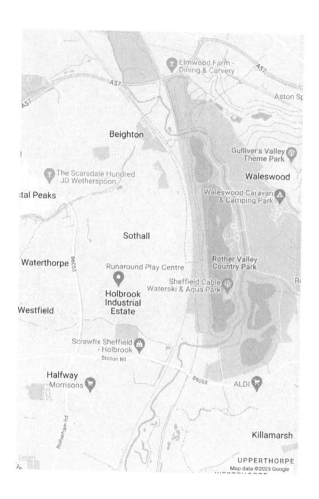

Sheffiel travel guide guide 2023-2024.

Map of Carbrook

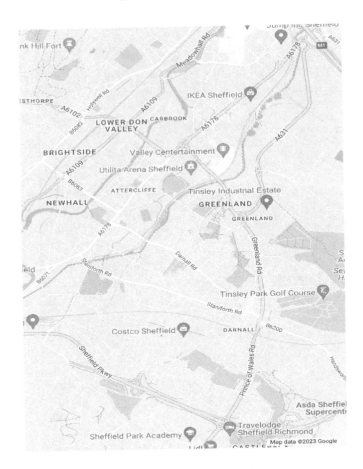

Map of Bradfield

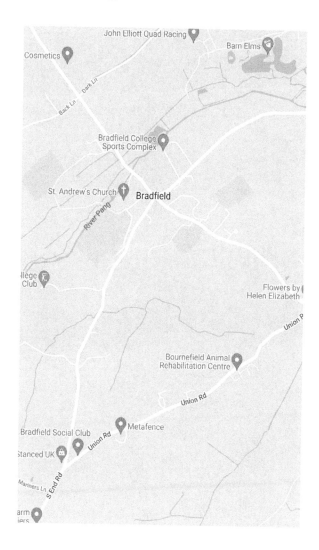

Sheffiel travel guide guide 2023-2024.

Map of Attercliffe

Table of Contents

Map of Beighton
Map of Carbrook
Map of Bradfield
Map of Attercliffe
Table of Contents
Chapter One
Introduction to Sheffield
   Overview of the City
   History of Sheffield
Chapter Two
Transportation in Sheffield
   Public transport
   Driving
   Walking
   5-DAY ITINERARY FOR YOU
   DAY 1
   DAY 2
   DAY 3
   DAY 4
   DAY 5
Chapter Three
Exploring Attractions
   Museums
   Parks
   Restaurants

Sheffiel travel guide guide 2023-2024.

Chapter Four
Local Local Culture
    Music
    Festivals and Events
Chapter Five
Where to Stay
    Hotels
    Bed and Breakfast
Chapter Six
Taking Care of Yourself
    Healthcare Resources
    Mental health
Chapter Seven
Living in Sheffield
    Cost of living
    Schooling
    Employment
Conclusion
    Replections on Sheffield
    Suggestions for Further Exploration

Chapter One

Introduction to Sheffield

I'd always been fascinated with Sheffield's history and culture. I'd heard of the city's vibrant cultural scene, steel industry, and role in the Industrial Revolution. I'd also heard about the city's magnificent parks and green spaces, as well as its proximity to the Peak District National Park.

So when the opportunity to work in Sheffield presented itself, I jumped at it. When I arrived in Sheffield in July, it was a cool and rainy day. Despite the bad weather, I was excited to explore the city.

Sheffiel travel guide guide 2023-2024.

My first trip was at the National Steel Museum. I learned about the history of Sheffield's steel industry and how it influenced the city's development. I also got to witness some of the remarkable equipment used to make steel in Sheffield.

Following the museum, I headed to the Crucible Theatre. Shakespeare's play was recently staged, with outstanding performance and production values.

The next day, I went for a walk in the Peak District National Park.I climbed one of the hills and was rewarded with stunning views of the city and the surrounding countryside.

I spent the rest of her trip seeing all of Sheffield's other ATTRACTIONS. I visited Sheffield Cathedral, Botanical

Gardens, and Winter Garden. In addition, I went shopping in the city's core and dined at some of its best restaurants.

By the time I had to go, I had fallen in love with Sheffield. I had grown to adore its natural beauty, culture, and history. I planned on returning at some point.

Overview of the City

Sheffield, located in northern England, is a prominent industrial, economic, and cultural centre. It has a rich and diverse history and was formerly part of the English county of South Yorkshire. Sheffield has been a prominent commercial and industrial city for decades, particularly during the nineteenth-century Industrial Revolution. Steel, courtesy of the Steelworks, has been the city's economic backbone.

Sheffield is now a pleasant, dynamic city with a variety of events that attract people of all ages and backgrounds. Sheffield, with a population of about 563,000, is one of the most important cities in the Midlands and the sixth-largest metropolitan area in England.

Culturally, Sheffield is known for its art galleries, theatres, music venues, and galleries. Visit the nearby Peace Gardens as well as the city's famous Millenium Galleries. There is a broad range of cafes and taverns, particularly in downtown and along the river.

Sheffield's athletic talent is well-known. Sheffield Wednesday Football Club is based in the city and is a big football enthusiast. The city also has world-class sporting facilities, including cricket, rugby league, and swimming pools.

Sheffiel travel guide guide 2023-2024.

Given its long history and diverse cultural offerings, it's easy to see why Sheffield is known as the "Steel City" by both inhabitants and visitors. There is something for everyone in Sheffield, including festivals, sporting events, and breathtaking natural and architectural treasures. Anyone looking for a great day or weekend getaway should go.

History of Sheffield

Sheffield's history, which began in a small Anglo-Saxon town, is complicated and spans thousands of years. As the principality of Mercia flourished and disintegrated, the territory around modern-day Sheffield quickly became a centre for commerce, industry, and political influence. Sheffield had an important role in British history beginning in the 11th century, participating in the Crusades as well as the growth and reform of the industrial sector.

Sheffield began as a tiny town in the ninth century and grew to become an important administrative centre in 1296. These lowly beginnings aided the city's rise to prominence, and in 1327 it was admitted to the Hanseatic League. The city's growth as an industrial powerhouse was fueled by the improved access to European markets made available by this.

Significant constructions from the era, such as Sheffield Castle, which was built in the 12th century, are still surviving today. This castle provided Sheffield with not just a stronghold of power, but also a sense of place and community. Sheffield's identity had been formed by the early to mid-15th century. Even now, historical structures such as the Old Town Hall remain as memories of this time of growth.

Sheffield had substantial expansion in the 16th and 17th centuries when the city was completely integrated into the English political structure. During these two centuries, the city gained two royal charters, and its population grew rapidly. This increase was caused by an influx of immigrant workers due to Sheffield's rising industrial production.

These immigrants contributed a substantial quantity of labour for the burgeoning industry during the early phases of the Industrial Revolution, considerably increasing the city's productivity and allowing it to develop into a key international trading port. During this time, the city's boundaries expanded significantly, and the city's infrastructure saw tremendous growth, including the installation of the first tramcars in 1883.

However, there were concerns with the industrial city's expansion as well. The air quality quickly worsened as haze engulfed the city center regularly. Following health difficulties, a catastrophic cholera pandemic erupted in 1832, claiming thousands of lives. Against all odds, the city overcame these difficulties, eventually transitioning into an era of working-class power and development.

Sheffield's thriving working communities are still making their mark today. Thanks to projects like the Meadowhall Shopping Centre, which opened in 1991, a new generation of workers who would otherwise have gone unemployed were offered chances. As part of the ambitious Heart of the City project, one of the most successful regeneration initiatives in the UK, the area around Barkers Pool and Fargate was renovated with new shops, offices, and apartments.

Sheffield has grown into a big city with a flourishing business and culture. The city welcomes tourists with several museums and galleries, as well as other cultural and historical landmarks. Sheffield is today a well-liked modern city with a promising future.

Chapter Two

Transportation in Sheffield

Public transport

Public transportation is critical to a city's or metropolis's health and efficiency. Sheffield, England's fourth-largest city, is no exception. Public transit is widely used in Sheffield and provides inhabitants with an efficient and frequently inexpensive form of mobility.

Sheffield's most common mode of public transportation is the Stagecoach bus system. The Sheffield Supertram, which debuted in 1994, is a light rail system that provides a local public transportation network to the city's most essential areas. The Supertram traverses 21 kilometres over six independent lines, from Meadowhall and Parkgate Retail World in the north to Cathedral and the hospitals in the west. Furthermore, the Supertram is linked to the bus system, giving maximum convenience.

Furthermore, Northern Rail and East Midlands Railway provide several rail lines that connect Sheffield with other major regional cities. There are also regular bus and rail links to London. Furthermore, Sheffield City Airport, which is 10 kilometres from the city and serves both domestic and international flights, makes it easy for people to get to and from Sheffield.

The South Yorkshire Passenger Transport Executive (SYPTE) is in charge of overseeing public transportation in Sheffield. They strive to make public transportation an appealing and ecologically responsible alternative for those who use it for commuting, pleasure, and work. SYPTE has negotiated lower fares for anyone who qualifies as a "concessionary passenger" to attain this aim. This includes children, students, and the elderly. SYPTE also oversees the Fit2Go program, which provides free tickets to people who want to become more physically active and encourages the use of public transportation, as well as walking, cycling, and public transit.

Sheffield's infrastructure includes a substantial quantity of public transit. Because of its effective and economical network, it is a desired and sustainable alternative to driving. Furthermore, initiatives such as the Fit2Go program and concessionary pricing ensure that everyone who needs mobility has access to it.

Sheffiel travel guide guide 2023-2024.

Driving

Sheffield's variety provides vehicles with multiple alternatives for navigating its streets and various-sized motorways. Its network of motorways, dual lanes, country roads, and city streets may provide an exciting journey, but each must be approached with caution. Before getting behind the wheel, prospective Sheffield drivers should get familiar with the city's myriad traffic laws and regulations.

The most crucial consideration while driving in Sheffield should be safety. Road conditions may be surprising, as they are in any city, therefore it is critical to be cautious at all times. They must obey all traffic signals, speed limits, and road signs if they wish to lessen their chances of an accident or injury. Furthermore, keeping a safe following distance is essential for retaining control of one's car. When driving, pedestrians, cyclists, and other drivers should all be paid additional attention.

In general, driving around Sheffield is a delight. On its many roads and terrain, there is something for drivers of all skill levels. Beautiful beauty, colourful culture, and unexpected road interactions are all benefits of cautious driving and following the rules. Driving in Sheffield allows you to explore and enjoy this dynamic city.

Walking

Sheffield, a flourishing English city amid the picturesque hills of North Yorkshire, is a hive of activity and history. Sheffield has had a special position in the hearts of both inhabitants and visitors since the Victorian period. Stepping within the city reveals instantly why it is so beloved. Sheffield is an excellent city for pedestrians due to its rich collection of culture, art, food, architecture, and green spaces.

Sheffield has a lot to offer anybody looking for a great walking adventure. The city centre is full of pedestrian-friendly lanes lined with bustling cafés, shops, and retailers. If you like exploring new areas, Sheffield has numerous possibilities for you. There are several routes you may take. Sheffield's parks and green spaces, such as the Botanical Gardens, Hillsborough Park, and Endcliffe Park, are great for a vigorous walk or a stroll.

Sheffield is a fantastic city for exploring on foot. It provides several health benefits in addition to enabling in-depth investigation of the city and its history. Walking has been shown to reduce stress, enhance physical fitness, cognitive performance, and even encourage emotional well-being.

Furthermore, it is an excellent chance to explore lesser-known places in greater Sheffield, such as the mediaeval Grenoside hamlet or the sumptuous St. Paul's Church on the city's western outskirts.

Sheffield is unquestionably a fantastic place for those who like going on walks. The plethora of guided tours in the city gives plenty of opportunities for exploration and storytelling to supplement your stroll. There are numerous knowledgeable and competent tour guides available to make your walk more interesting and amusing, whether it's a historical or cultural trip. Visit Sheffield, on the other hand, provides a choice of touring trails to ensure that you do not miss any of Sheffield's countless unknown sites if you want to explore on your own.

All of these characteristics combine to make walking in Sheffield a pleasurable and rewarding experience. There are several opportunities to uncover unique sites and hidden surprises across the city. Sheffield can surely satisfy those looking for an excellent walking experience. Sheffield differentiates itself as one of the best cities in England for pedestrian exploration by capitalising on its lively streets, parks, culture, and history.

5-DAY ITINERARY FOR YOU

DAY 1

MORNING

First thing in the morning, go to the magnificent Sheffield Botanical Gardens. A leisurely stroll through the wonderfully maintained gardens is an excellent chance to appreciate the variety of plants and flowers on display.

Sheffiel travel guide guide 2023-2024.

AFTERNOON

After you've toured the gardens, go to the Millennium Gallery in the heart of Sheffield. This museum has a mix of interactive displays and art, design, and craft shows. The metalwork show, which depicts Sheffield's rich industrial past, is not to be missed.

Bedtime. Find fantastic Sheffield lodging.

EVENING

For dinner, go to The Milestone, a well-known restaurant known for its fresh British fare. Enjoy the locally sourced ingredients in their food and their extensive wine collection.

DAY 2

MORNING

Sheffield Cathedral is a wonderful example of Gothic design and should be seen first thing in the morning. Taking a guided tour of the cathedral allows you to learn about its history while viewing its spectacular stained glass windows.

AFTERNOON

Following your tour to the chapel, pay a visit to the Kelham Island Museum, which is located in a former industrial area. Sheffield's steelmaking tradition is celebrated in this museum, which depicts the story of the city's industrial past. Investigate the fascinating exhibitions to learn about the innovations that shaped Sheffield's history.

Bedtime. Find fantastic Sheffield lodging.

EVENING

Treat yourself to a delicious meal at Jöro, a modern bistro known for its innovative and environmentally friendly dining concept. The menu's utilisation of seasonal ingredients and innovative dishes will impress any culinary lover.

DAY 3

MORNING

Spend the morning touring the Peak District National Park, which is located near Sheffield. While hiking or bicycling through the picturesque countryside, take in the breathtaking views. Don't forget to bring food for a picnic in one of the park's most lovely areas.

AFTERNOON

After your outdoor adventure, go to the Sheffield Winter Garden, a large glasshouse with plants from all over the world. Take a leisurely stroll in the garden to enjoy its tranquillity.
Bedtime. Find fantastic Sheffield lodging.

EVENING

Make a reservation for dinner at Silversmiths, a restaurant known for its modern British cuisine. While taking in the comfortable atmosphere of the restaurant, enjoy cuisine cooked with locally produced products.

DAY 4

MORNING

The Sheffield Antiques Quarter, a lively neighbourhood filled with antique shops and vintage boutiques, is an excellent place to begin your day. Spend some time searching over the strange items; you could find something special to take home.

AFTERNOON

After visiting the Antiques Quarter, continue on to the Sheffield Industrial Heritage Trail. This self-guided tour takes you through Sheffield's industrial past, highlighting major places and structures in the city's history.
Bedtime. Find fantastic Sheffield lodging.

EVENING

Dinner at The Old House, a popular pub known for its friendly atmosphere and broad craft beer menu, is a terrific way to end the day. Relax in the lovely surroundings while enjoying traditional British pub grub with a modern touch.

DAY 5

MORNING

Visit the Sheffield Peace Gardens first thing in the morning for a peaceful sanctuary in the heart of the city. Spend some time relaxing and observing the beautiful sculptures and fountains.

AFTERNOON

After touring the Peace Gardens, visit the Kelham Island Brewery and drink some beer. The brewing process will be discussed, and delicious beers will be served.

Bedtime. Find fantastic Sheffield lodging.

EVENING

For supper, head to Rafters, a Michelin-starred restaurant known for its complex and inventive cuisine. While indulging in the exquisite setting of the restaurant, enjoy a tasting menu featuring the greatest British ingredients.

Chapter Three

Exploring Attractions

Museums

Museums of Sheffield is a collection of 15 museums located around Sheffield, England. Visitors are urged to explore the local museums to learn more about the history of the city and its surroundings. Kelham Island Museum, for example, focuses on the industrial revolution, whilst Weston Park Museum is dedicated to the Victorian era. Furthermore, Abbeydale Industrial Hamlet examines the lives of local employees.

The Endcliffe Park Visitor Center, on the other hand, displays the park's history in the terrain during the nineteenth century.

Sheffield Town Hall Museum serves as the municipal museum for Sheffield City Council. A variety of exhibitions greet visitors inside, exploring the city's history and legacy from its origins as an agricultural village in the Middle Ages to the present. Artwork, furniture, shop fittings, and antiques from various eras of Sheffield's history may be found here.

Meanwhile, the artist and philosopher John Ruskin is being celebrated at the Ruskin Gallery. It includes his drawings, sculptures, paintings, and prose. Some of his significant works are also highlighted in the connected Ruskin Library. For anyone interested in learning more about his life and work, the museum conducts regular educational programs such as lectures, seminars, and walks.

Additional museums in Sheffield include the Millennium Gallery, which specialises in metalwork, jewellery, and ceramics, the

Graves Art Gallery, which houses an impressive collection of foreign and British works of art, and the Keepers Cottage Museum, which houses a variety of regional historical and natural history collections. Sheffield also features museums dedicated to certain topics such as railroading, technology, and medicine.

These informative and interactive museums are ideal for travellers of all ages who wish to learn more about the city, its history, culture, and people. Every visitor is guaranteed a colourful and memorable experience. Given Sheffield's vibrant museum culture, it's simple to understand why these museums are so popular. They are critical to preserving the city's particular heritage and history for future generations.

Parks

Sheffield is known for its diverse natural beauty and lengthy history. Sheffield offers a fantastic collection of parks, green spaces, and gardens that provide residents and visitors with a wide range of recreational options. From well-known parks like Endcliffe and Graves to lesser-known gems like Manor Field and Old Edwardians, Sheffield's parks provide opportunities for exercise, sports, exploration, and relaxation.

Endcliffe Park is a massive 54-acre expanse of lovely meadows and grassland at the foot of the peak region. As guests reach the region, they are greeted with the huge ruins of Endcliffe Hall, a Grade II listed edifice set atop a hill and affording a great perspective of the park below. Tennis courts, playgrounds for children, and jogging paths are among the various activities accessible at the park. The four lakes that dot the park are likewise stunningly gorgeous and attract a diverse range of wildlife.

Meanwhile, Graves Park is home to many attractions. With its lovely gardens, open green spaces, forests, and woodland wildflower meadows, it provides a nice location for picnics, cycling, and soaking in the stunning lakeside views for both inhabitants and tourists. Other attractions in the park include a seasonal boating lake, an animal farm, and outdoor theatres.

Manor Field may be Sheffield's best-kept secret. This serene park exemplifies the special charm of the city's green spaces by being home to a diverse range of flora and fauna. The park, which is ideally placed in the town centre, provides easy access to a network of walkways that allow visitors to enjoy the wonders of nature. Finally, Old Edwardians Park is a smaller but gorgeous park with a lot of open green spaces, a duck pond, and a variety of playgrounds.

Sheffield is recognized for its various parks and outdoor spaces, which range from more quiet and lesser-known areas such as Manor Field and Old Edwardians to historic parks such as Endcliffe and Graves. Each of these green spaces allows residents and visitors to experience all Sheffield has to offer. Sheffield's parks provide something special for everyone to enjoy, whether it's for exercise, exploration, or just resting.

Restaurants

Sheffield, with its booming city, is a fascinating site for any dining experience. Visitors to Sheffield have a broad range of culinary options to choose from, including Michelin-starred restaurants and family-run establishments.

The Piccolino Restaurant in Sheffield is a well-known fine dining establishment. The Piccolino, built in a historic Victorian gatehouse, provides a refined atmosphere with renowned chefs' modern Italian food. Among the menu's highlights are gourmet pizzas, Grana Padano, and freshly made pasta. The nearby Caffè Bar serves Italian-style coffees, pastries, and sandwiches.

If you want something more casual, the Rocca Café is a great choice. The café, located on Ecclesall Road in Sheffield, provides a broad menu of globally inspired dishes with a focus on natural and seasonal ingredients. The menu changes daily, but favourites include quinoa and kale vegetable bowls, hake with walnut crust, and a range of local cheeses. There are also vegan and gluten-free alternatives available in the café.

The Erewash Inn is a reliable gastropub in Sheffield's Broomhall district for those who like traditional British cooking. The menu features traditional English pub fare such as fish and chips, bangers and mash, and shepherd's pie. The bar also has a selection of fine wines from across the world as well as local ales on tap.

Last, but not least, The Botanist is a unique restaurant in the City Center with an outdoor atmosphere. The Botanist, which features a rooftop terrace, offers seasonal outdoor dining experiences using fresh herbs, fruits, and vegetables from the nearby Botanical Gardens. The menu includes a variety of dishes ranging from wood-fired pizzas and homemade kinds of pasta to delicate steaks and fresh seafood, with an emphasis on global cuisines.

To summarise, Sheffield is an excellent destination for foodies of all tastes. Sheffield has alternatives for every taste and budget, whether you want a classy dining experience, something more casual, or typical pub cuisine. Sheffield's many dining options ensure that every visitor has a memorable dining experience.

Chapter Four

Local Local Culture

Music

Sheffield has long been recognized for its diverse music scene. Since the late 1970s, Sheffield has been the epicentre of punk, electronic, and dance music, giving birth to sub-genres such as 'Bleep and Bass' in the 1980s and Sheffield Grime in the 2000s. The DJs, performers, and venues that comprise Sheffield's music scene are responsible for the city's unique sound.

Punk rock acts such as the Human League, ABC, Heaven 17, Siouxsie and the Banshees, and Def Leppard dominated the Sheffield music scene in the late 1970s and early 1980s. By the mid-1980s, the post-punk sound had begun to permeate over the airways and take on a particularly Sheffield Ian flavour. This began the city's electronic music scene, which has since risen to prominence. Human League and Heaven 17 established the electro-pop sound in the region, and well-known musicians like Aphex Twin, Squarepusher, Pearson Sound, and Simian Mobile Disco were impacted by the genre's growth.

Sheffield is recognized as being the home of British dance music due to the introduction of new labels like Warp Records to encourage local artists. As a consequence of Bleep and Bass, producers like LFO, Nightmares on Wax, Global Communication, and Richie Hawtin achieved popularity in Sheffield's electronic music scene. The city's techno and electronic music sectors, as well as the dance music culture, were heavily impacted by British rap, as were the city's nightclubs and house parties. Moloko, a well-known and popular local rap group, also paid a visit to the nightclubs in Sheffield. De La Soul, an American rapper, also performed there.

Bassline is a fast-paced, bass-heavy music genre that became popular in Sheffield dance venues around the year 2000. DJs like

Toddla T, Sandeeno, and DJ Marky helped to establish Bassline's name in the city. The influence of Bassline can still be heard today, and the genre evolved through several variations before reaching the modern Sheffield Grime sound.

Although rap, hip-hop, and grime currently dominate Sheffield's airwaves, there is still room for other genres to flourish. Some of the city's taverns and clubs still maintain vibrant jazz, folk, and acoustic music scenes, encouraging local performers to join the established electronic music sector. Sheffield's recording studios have been able to invest in cutting-edge technology and support not just electronic music but also other genres with the advent of the Gatecrasher nightclub in the 1990s.

The range of music created in Sheffield today reflects the musical community's diversity. The city's networks of music venues, promoters, labels, DJs, and performers have grown and changed throughout time, and although the music business in Sheffield has changed, it is still flourishing today. Sheffield is a hub for avant-garde and one-of-a-kind music, and it remains a worldwide music scene leader.

Festivals and Events

Sheffield, a northern English industrial city, is known for its diversified population and culture. There are several festivals and events hosted there, ranging from the city's traditional fairs and parades to well-known music festivals and concerts. In this article, we will look at the various festivals and events held in Sheffield, using examples from the city's long and illustrious cultural past.

The Whit Walks are the oldest, dating back to 1439 and celebrating Sheffield's past. From May through mid-summer, many Whit Walks are organised across the city. Historical games, bonfires, and a stunning fireworks display create a joyful atmosphere as residents dress in mediaeval garb and march to the rhythm of a drum corps.

The Bramall Lane Festival, which takes place in September, is another popular event in Sheffield. At this event, the local community comes together to enjoy unique music, which is based on a love of innovative and varied musical genres. Local, national, and international recording artists perform throughout the venue's four stages. There are also food and drink vendors, art installations, and dance acts during the event.

Sheffield, in addition to its flourishing music scene, has several annual street fairs, including the Walkley Arts and Crafts Fair and the Moor Arts and Crafts Fair. These events provide both local and visiting artisans an opportunity to showcase their work to the public. Both events include a range of talks and performances, handmade artisan booths, and food trucks providing a variety of international cuisines.

Sheffield Eats Street Food Festival is a culinary experience for foodies that takes place every September. This event features the finest of the city's wares. Street food vendors, food trucks, and pop-up eateries provide anything from tacos and burgers to noodles and pop-up restaurants. The festival includes a variety of entertainment selections as well as family-friendly activities.

The Great Yorkshire Fringe Festival has grown in prominence in Sheffield since its inception in 2016. This unique event, held in July, brings together the top performers from the West End and beyond, as well as the best of the fringe scene. Performers bring comedy, music, and dramatic events to audiences in unexpected venues.

The Four Square Festival is another wonderful example of the diversity of Sheffield's activities. The festival celebrates contemporary art and music by showcasing a diverse mix of well-known and new artists from across the world. A variety of venues host performances, installations, live readings, and film screenings, promoting a creative, vibrant atmosphere.

Last but not least, in June, the Sheffield Mela brings together art, music, dance, and gastronomy from all over the world. The inclusion of street performers, DJs, live music, and dance groups from all over the globe creates a unique and dynamic setting.

Sheffield's several events, ranging from Whit Walks to Sheffield Eats Street Food Festival, demonstrate the city's dynamic and creative spirit. Sheffield has a superb selection of traditions, events, and performances, so there's no excuse not to take advantage of them all.

Chapter Five

Where to Stay

Hotels

Sheffield, , is a very bustling metropolis. It is a popular tourist destination with a range of hotels to accommodate visitors from all walks of life. In this post, we'll look at the many hotel classifications available in Sheffield, as well as the unique services each one provides.

Sheffield's hotel sector is quite diverse and varied. For those looking for more lavish accommodations, one of the city's several full-service hotels may be an alternative. The majority of these properties provide all of the amenities one would expect from a high-end hotel, such as suites with private balconies, luxurious design, complimentary continental breakfast, first-rate service, and access to the on-site spa, pool, and fitness center. Sheffield also has a variety of boutique and low-cost hotels, including bed and breakfasts and small independent inns.

Regardless of the kind of housing they pick, visitors to Sheffield can count on a broad choice of wonderful amenities. Several hotels provide complimentary shuttle services to and from the airport and railway station, as well as city tours, for guests who wish to explore the city's distinguishing attractions. Furthermore, Sheffield's hotels provide handy on-site amenities such as business centres, concierge services, and laundry facilities to assist guests to stay connected and productive while travelling.

When searching for a hotel in Sheffield, one should consider their desires and expectations. All sorts of travellers may find a place to stay in the city, whether they're looking for a comfortable spot to sleep at night or luxury seekers looking for the red-carpet treatment. The best hotel for every client will therefore be determined entirely by their financial circumstances, chosen amenities, and overall wants.

Sheffield offers a wide range of housing options for travellers, ranging from lavish full-service hotels to more inexpensive bed and breakfasts. Whatever one's budget, it is easy to choose the appropriate hotel to meet individual wants and expectations. With the diversity of options available, travellers are certain to find the appropriate spot for their stay in Sheffield.

Here are four best low cost Hotels For You

1.The easyHotel in Sheffield City Centre.

The Peace Gardens and the train station are both just a short walk from our hotel in the heart of Sheffield. It offers simple, functional lodgings with all the amenities, including complimentary Wi-Fi.

Sheffiel travel guide guide 2023-2024.

2.Sheffield Arena hotel on a budget

. This hotel is close to the Sheffield Arena and the Don Valley Stadium. It offers free Wi-Fi, breakfast, and modern, comfortable accommodations.

3.Ibis Sheffield Centre St. Mary's Gate

is a low-cost hotel. Both the Winter Garden and the train station are close to this hotel's city centre position. It provides elegant, contemporary accommodations with free Wi-Fi and breakfast.

4.Sheffield's central Travelodge.

The Peace Gardens and the train station are both just a short walk from our hotel in the heart of Sheffield. It offers comfortable, fully equipped rooms with free WiFi.

Bed and Breakfast

Sheffield is wonderfully hidden in the heart of the United Kingdom. This lovely English city in South Yorkshire County is well-known for its abundance of green areas, including parks and gardens, as well as its long history of manufacturing and industry. One of the many elements that lure visitors to Sheffield is the diversity of bed and breakfast (B&B) accommodations.

Bed and breakfasts in Sheffield provide travellers with a unique experience and more personalised hospitality than other types of housing. B&Bs provide welcoming surroundings that make tourists feel at home, in addition to providing a range of facilities such as comfy beds, air conditioning, fitness centres, and unique access to adjacent attractions. The city's bed and breakfasts often collaborate with nearby businesses, allowing them to provide discounts on nearby facilities and services.

Bed & breakfasts in Sheffield have long supplied tourists with a warm home away from home. Because of their private rooms, facilities, and educated local information, they ensure that guests may rest and enjoy their stay. Many of the city's attractions, such as the vibrant music and nightlife scenes, are accessible to Sheffield B&B visitors.

Over the past several years, the city's bed and breakfast sector has grown in both size and prominence. Sheffield's bed and breakfasts are attracting increasing visitors of all kinds as people seek unique and authentic housing options. Sheffield B&Bs provide something for everyone, from couples looking for a relaxing holiday to families looking for thrill and adventure.

Sheffield's Bed and Breakfasts have gradually enhanced the quality of their services. To remain competitive in the face of increased competition, owners have had to improve their game. B&Bs work hard to give tourists everything they want, including high-quality furnishings and warm hospitality.

Bed and breakfast accommodation is growing increasingly popular in Sheffield. Sheffield is ideal for guests searching for a unique holiday experience due to its diverse housing options, welcoming setting, and attention to detail. Sheffield B&Bs provide something for everyone, whether you're looking for adventure or a change of scenery.

Sheffiel travel guide guide 2023-2024.

Chapter Six

Taking Care of Yourself

Healthcare Resources

Sheffield, has great healthcare services. Despite being a member of the United Kingdom's National Health Service (NHS), Sheffield stands apart for the sheer amount of healthcare services it provides in both the city core and the outlying boroughs. This research will evaluate and assess the medical facilities, services, and initiatives available in the city and its neighboring boroughs.

Sheffield is home to six major hospitals. Charles Clifford, Royal Hallamshire, Northern General, Weston Park, Jessop Wing, and Claremont are among them. The Royal Hallamshire Hospital, the largest of these six, serves more than 450,000 people in Sheffield and the surrounding South Yorkshire area. It provides diagnostic and therapeutic services in medicine, surgery, and dentistry, as well as emergency and urgent care services. Northern General Hospital, Sheffield's second-largest hospital, provides a wide range of medical services, from accident and emergency care to specialised surgery. Weston Park Hospital provides high-dose-rate brachytherapy, chemotherapy, and radiation treatment for cancer patients, while the Jessop Wing concentrates on maternity care and other women's health services. Claremont Hospital specialises in treating mental health difficulties, whilst Charles Clifford handles patients who are blind or visually impaired.

Sheffield has other medical facilities in addition to these six hospitals. The city has several healthcare institutions that provide treatment and help for a range of conditions. These clinics provide general care for minor ailments, as well as nutritionists, mental health support, and addiction treatment programs. The Pathology Network provides diagnostic services in Sheffield, while the Sheffield Teaching Hospitals NHS Foundation Trust oversees numerous community hospitals in the city's poorest districts.

Furthermore, the area is home to various nonprofit healthcare centres that offer further medical treatment, support, and assistance. The Sheffield Children's Hospital Charity, for example, aims to improve the quality of life for young patients as well as the lives of children in the community. The Sheffield branch of the Macmillan Cancer help organisation offers crucial help to cancer patients, ranging from emotional support to practical assistance such as financial counselling. The Sue Ryder Neurological Treatment Charitable Trust, with a facility at the Royal Hallamshire Hospital, provides professional treatment and help to persons suffering from neurological issues.

These charitable organisations not only help to enhance Sheffield's healthcare standards but also represent the city's strong sense of community. Residents of the city work together to help and protect one another as much as they can, building the foundations for a strong foundation of universal health care.

Finally, Sheffield has enough healthcare resources. It has six large hospitals that provide a wide range of medical services, as well as various health clinics and charitable organisations that provide further assistance and support. These resources, when combined, provide everyone in Sheffield access to high-quality healthcare, reflecting the city's commitment to good health.

Mental health

Because of the rapid advancement of technology and globalisation, mental health has garnered more attention in recent years. As a result of this greater understanding, local governments must immediately recognize their inhabitants' mental health needs and provide the resources necessary to meet those needs. The purpose of this article is to investigate the extent to which mental health issues have spread in Sheffield, UK, as well as the efficacy of legal reforms in tackling them.

According to a study, psychological and emotional diseases have progressively developed in Sheffield during the previous 10 years. According to a 2016 National Health Service study, the number of people in the city who have been diagnosed with anxiety or depression has climbed by 13% since 2011, which is greater than the national average of 8%. Furthermore, the estimated lifetime prevalence of diagnosable mental illness is 17%, 5% higher than the national norm. This has been attributed to a variety of factors, including the city's significant poverty, inequality, and unemployment rates.

As a result, policymakers in Sheffield and the surrounding areas have taken significant steps to mitigate the effects of mental health concerns. One measure was the 2011 unveiling of the "Health and

Wellbeing Strategy," which aimed to give funds and aid to persons suffering from mental illnesses. This strategy involves the establishment of Mental Health Trusts, which are dedicated to providing mental health treatment to all Sheffield citizens. Furthermore, local charities and foundations offer financial and emotional assistance to those in need, while local groups such as the Samaritans provide mental health support and counselling.

In addition to legislative action, the public sector has funded awareness campaigns aimed at destigmatizing mental health and eliminating any underlying stigma connected with its discussion. As a result, more schools and universities are participating in the dialogue, and those educational institutions are promoting mental health services and resources. In addition, Sheffield has hosted numerous events that promote open discussion and debate on mental health, such as the

"Mental Health Awareness Week" and "Walking for Mental Health" campaigns.

Overall, Sheffield's mental health status has deteriorated considerably in recent years, with an increasing number of citizens reporting mental health illnesses. However, government policy initiatives, grassroots campaigns, and outreach programs have shown to be beneficial in serving the needs of the general public. As a result, to dramatically modify the region's mental health environment, politicians and the public sector must maintain their efforts to provide mental health services and education.

Chapter Seven

Living in Sheffield

Cost of living

Sheffield has a high cost of living, necessitating careful consideration. Although living in Sheffield might be costly, there are ways to save money if you plan ahead of time. This article will look at the cost of living in Sheffield, compare it to other British cities, and provide practical suggestions on how to do so on a budget.

The cost of living in England varies tremendously depending on region and city, and Sheffield is no exception. To get a realistic sense of how much it could cost to live in Sheffield, consider all of the aspects that influence the cost of living, such as housing, transportation, education, healthcare, and food expenditures.

Housing

A one-bedroom apartment in Sheffield's city centre normally costs £663 per month to rent. This cost is higher than the national average of £575 per month. A three-bedroom apartment in the city centre would cost roughly £1,159 per month. Renting an apartment outside of the city centre is often less costly.

Transportation

A single ticket for Sheffield's public transportation system costs roughly £2.40. There are also monthly travel cards available for as low as £99. Cycling is another option for those who wish to get to Sheffield quickly and cheaply. Sheffield has an extensive network of bike paths.

Sheffiel travel guide guide 2023-2024.

Education

Another factor to consider when calculating how much it would cost to live in Sheffield is education. Three universities and other continuing education colleges are located in the city, with yearly tuition for in-state students ranging from about £9,000.

Healthcare

Another part of city living expenses is the cost of healthcare. The public National Health Service (NHS) provides free healthcare to all British people. There are more private healthcare choices, which may be more expensive.

Groceries

The cost of living includes grocery expenditures. Food is frequently moderately priced in the city, with possible savings when purchased in bulk and at adjacent farmer's markets. In Sheffield, basic consumables generally cost about £250 per month.

Sheffield's overall cost of living is higher than the national average, yet there are ways to save money. By carefully analysing the costs of housing, transportation, education, healthcare, and food, you may find a balance that works for you and allows you to live in Sheffield inexpensively.

Schooling

Sheffield recognizes the value of education and is proud to offer its inhabitants a world-class education. The city is well-known for its prestigious educational facilities and highly qualified professors. However, several difficulties must be addressed before Sheffield citizens can get a high-quality education. This essay will look at the possibilities and challenges of the Sheffield educational system.

Sheffield offers a wide range of high-quality educational options to its citizens. The distinction between primary and secondary education is significant, with elementary school containing courses like arithmetic and physics, as well as English and the arts. Sheffield is also home to six universities. These are intellectual study centres that provide lessons in a variety of subjects ranging from engineering to economics.

Another notable feature of Sheffield's educational system is the quality of its teachers. Teachers' educational backgrounds range from Bachelor's and Master's degrees to PHDs and beyond. This degree of educational competence is supported by a complex educational system that fosters open communication between instructors and students and allows teachers to get up-to-date training and information.

Despite these advantages, Sheffield's educational system continues to face challenges. The most visible of them is a lack of social inclusion. While Leeds and Manchester may have higher rates of educational attainment, Sheffield has been chastised for failing to foster social inclusion. There are still huge variations in educational experiences across socioeconomic classes, and the city has high levels of poverty and inequality.

Sheffield's educational system is also impoverished. Budget cuts at the federal and municipal levels have reduced financing and support for educational programs, and the city now faces a scarcity of part-time learning options. These financial challenges have influenced the quality of education in the city, forcing some learning establishments to shut down.

Sheffield's educational system has both positive and negative aspects. On the other hand, the city boasts a wealth of outstanding educational opportunities as well as a highly trained teaching staff. On the negative side, the city's educational system has stalled owing to a lack of socioeconomic inclusion and inadequate funding. Although change will be slow and difficult, Sheffield may be able to deliver the degree of education it seeks with extra funds and help. Sheffield's school system will remain untrustworthy till then.

Employment

Sheffield is supported by a variety of notable enterprises and industries. The advanced engineering, manufacturing, retail, health, education, engineering, and construction industries employ the majority of Sheffield residents. According to the Office for National Statistics, there will be around 250,000 employees in Sheffield by mid-2020, as well as approximately 35,000 self-employed persons.

One of the most amazing elements of Sheffield's work situation is that it has had the highest net job creation in Yorkshire and the Humber over the previous 10 years. This is due in part to the city's commitment to embracing cutting-edge technology and its growing student population. The establishment of offices by large technology businesses such as Bentley Systems, Creative-Lease, Cascade Enterprising, and PlusNet Technologies has provided numerous job opportunities for the locals. With around 44,000 students enrolling in 2020-21, the University of Sheffield has also made a substantial contribution to the area's employment rate. The institution helps the local economy in a variety of ways, including knowledge transfer, research partnerships, and other relevant initiatives.

The retail industry contributes considerably to Sheffield's employment environment since several large enterprises have established themselves in the city, including the Meadowhall Shopping Center, BHS, Sainsbury's, Marks & Spencer, and ASDA. With 164 stores in the Meadowhall Shopping Centre alone, these firms have lately produced a substantial number of job vacancies in the city. Other firms with positions for part-time or temporary workers include Oxfam, Habitat, and the University of Sheffield's campus store.

The wholesale, retail, and automotive trades business, which employs over 34,000 people in the Sheffield area, is a large employer. Manufacturing is another major employer, employing over 40,000 people. A substantial number of these manufacturing jobs are in the steel, medical device, car, aerospace, and chemical industries, as well as other allied industries. Because of the city's high concentration of advanced engineering, several of these vocations offer above-average wages.

Overall, Sheffield's labor market is active and diverse, offering a wide range of job opportunities in several sectors. In addition to the aforementioned industries, Sheffield is home to some other professions that provide a wide range of job opportunities, such as banking and finance, tourism and hospitality, and the creative and digital industries. Sheffield's diverse work climate demonstrates the city's continued commitment to offering job opportunities for its inhabitants.

Sheffiel travel guide guide 2023-2024.

Conclusion

Reflections on Sheffield

Considerations on Sheffield is an eye-catching and underappreciated British city. Sheffield, in the northwest of England, offers a vibrant cultural environment, beautiful natural surroundings, and a unique global outlook. Investigating Sheffield's specific character may teach us significant lessons about the history and culture of England as a whole.

Since the beginning of the industrial revolution, Sheffield has been a focal point. It was well-known for producing cutlery, armament, and other metal items, mainly steel and iron. Sheffield quickly came to prominence during the Industrial Revolution, both inside the British Isles and internationally, as a consequence of its manufacturers' supply of raw materials critical to the worldwide rise of industry.

Sheffield has transformed into a 21st-century development hub. It is the epicentre of a thriving IT industry, with corporations like IBM, Siemens, and Amazon establishing themselves here. Sheffield has developed from its industrial history to become a cutting-edge city with an emphasis on the arts and culture. Sheffield's streets are densely packed with small boutiques and cafés, in addition to some well-known landmarks such as the Sheffield Winter Garden and Town Hall.

The city is also recognized for its parks and gardens, which can be found throughout the suburbs and city centre. Hills, reservoirs, rivers, and the surrounding countryside are all conveniently accessible from Sheffield, a city that has traditionally valued nature. Sheffielders have always had a special passion for nature, whether it's hiking through the Peak District or playing golf on one of the city's many golf courses.

Sheffield has welcomed both diversity and multiculturalism. Today, the city is home to over 145 unique ethnic groups speaking over 100 languages. This worldwide awareness and the city's cosmopolitan feel have resulted in a particular understanding of the world and human interaction.

Last but not least, Sheffield is a living representation of England's convoluted history. Sheffield has been an important industrial centre since the 17th century, and the city's factories, workshops, and enormous steelworks serve as a continual reminder of Sheffield's prominence in British history. Sheffield's streets and buildings still give evidence of the city's history.

By researching Sheffield, we may learn more about the culture, history, and character of Sheffield and the British Isles as a whole. We may also learn more about how industrial civilizations emerged over much of the modern world. Furthermore, we can see how Sheffield's embrace of both nature and diversity has led to the development of a unique and vibrant culture that has influenced this part of England.

Sheffiel travel guide guide 2023-2024.

Suggestions for Further Exploration

Sheffield is a popular tourist destination for both locals and visitors from other countries. Sheffield offers something for everyone, with a rich industrial history, a thriving arts and music scene, and plenty of natural beauty. Those that take the time to explore the city will discover a variety of activities and attractions, ranging from parks and museums to shopping and eating options. There is, however, a lot more available for those who wish to continue exploring Sheffield.

The National Environmental Research Council, the Institute of Structural and Molecular Biology, and the Centre for Environment, Fisheries, and Aquaculture Science are among the research institutes and organisations based in Sheffield. Each of these institutes offers opportunities for learning and discovery as their research teams seek answers to difficult environmental or biological concerns. Visitors may participate in interesting talks and lectures with representatives from these organisations, as well as fieldwork and research for a unique experience.

Sheffield's past has also played an important influence in establishing who it is now. A visit to the city is required for anybody with an interest in history. The city has several historical sites, such as the Weston Park Museum, the Kelham Island Industrial Museum, and other 19th-century palaces and structures. A visit to these locations will help you better understand Sheffield's unique history and development, as well as its people.

For artistic individuals, Sheffield offers a variety of music, arts, and culture-related events and activities. Visitors may immerse themselves in the unique local art scene by visiting art galleries, music venues, and movie theatres. The city boasts a flourishing theatrical industry, with regular performances by both local performers and major touring companies.

Finally, every trip to Sheffield must include a visit to the great outdoors. Sheffield is bordered by several national parks, animal preserves, and scenic walks, therefore it is rich in natural beauty. For those searching for a little adventure, local enterprises offer rock climbing, kayaking, and other activities.

Sheffield is a location worth investigating. A trip to the city is certain to be enjoyable and instructive, with a wide range of activities to appeal to a wide range of interests. Anyone visiting Sheffield should plan a longer stay to take advantage of all the sights and activities that this great city has to offer.

Sheffiel travel guide guide 2023-2024.

Thanks Thanks for Reading,

Hope to see you in another

book

Happy Reading!

Printed in Great Britain
by Amazon

28509480R00050